love letters.

By
Ezana Salgado

Illustrated By
Elliana Esquivel

Love Letters
New York, NY 10010

Copyright © 2020 by Ezana Salgado

Design by Rodrigo Corral Studio

Book Interior Design Managing: Hsu + Associates
Book Interior Design Assistant: Megan Lee

Printed in USA

2022 2023 2024 2025 / 10 9 8 7 6 5 4 3 2 1

ISBN: 9798809890779

Facebook.com/loveletters
Twitter: @loveletters
Instagram.com/loveletters
Pinterest.com/loveletters
Youtube.com/user/loveletters
Issuu.com/loveletters

if you love her,
if you really love her,
you will do anything
to be with her.

you don't have to be
perfect for me to
love you, i'll love
you no matter what.

loving you
is my safe
place.

you're my best friend, and
lover, the only one
i want, you're all
that matters.

don't chase him, when
a man loves you, there's
nothing he wouldn't do
to be with you.

never beg for his
love. he should
offer it with
both arms open.

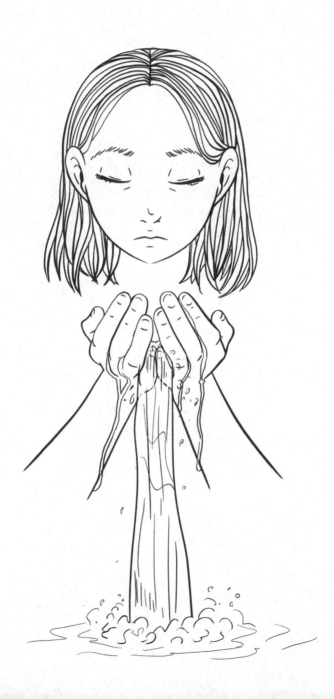

a man who says he
needs time to figure
out if he loves you,
has already given you
his answer.

i don't remember exactly
when it was, the moment
i fell in love with
you, but i do know it's
a feeling i'll never
forget.

don't waste time
on a man who
doesn't see your
worth.

a man who loves
you, will never
let you forget how
important you are.

if she asks questions
it means she cares,
and if she cares it
means she loves you.

find a man who
doesn't blame you
for his mistakes.

he wasn't capable
of loving the way
you loved. it's
not your fault.

she wants you
to make an effort,
to show her that
you care.

don't give him
your heart if he
doesn't deserve
it, darling.

darling, you
are all i ever
wanted love
to be.

"what's the matter?"

"i just want to feel beautiful. like the world doesn't hate me for who i am."

 "darling, can i just tell you, you are the most beautiful person i have ever met. and i truly mean that."

"why do you think i'm beautiful?"

"oh there's a million reasons. when i look at you i feel like you are my whole world. like every feeling i have ever felt and ever will feel is somehow connected with you. i love you like no one will ever know because i have never felt this kind of love. without you my heart would not be whole and i wouldn't know what to do. darling, look at me... without you my heart would be broken. i may eventually find my way back, but everything would be dark. like all the light had been taken from the world."

(she started crying)

"but i feel like you... like you shouldn't think of me that way..."

(he took her hand)

"darling, as long as i have you... i will love you forever. i promise. okay?"

find a man who doesn't
make you feel like you
have to compete with
other women.

she didn't
need to be fixed,
just loved.

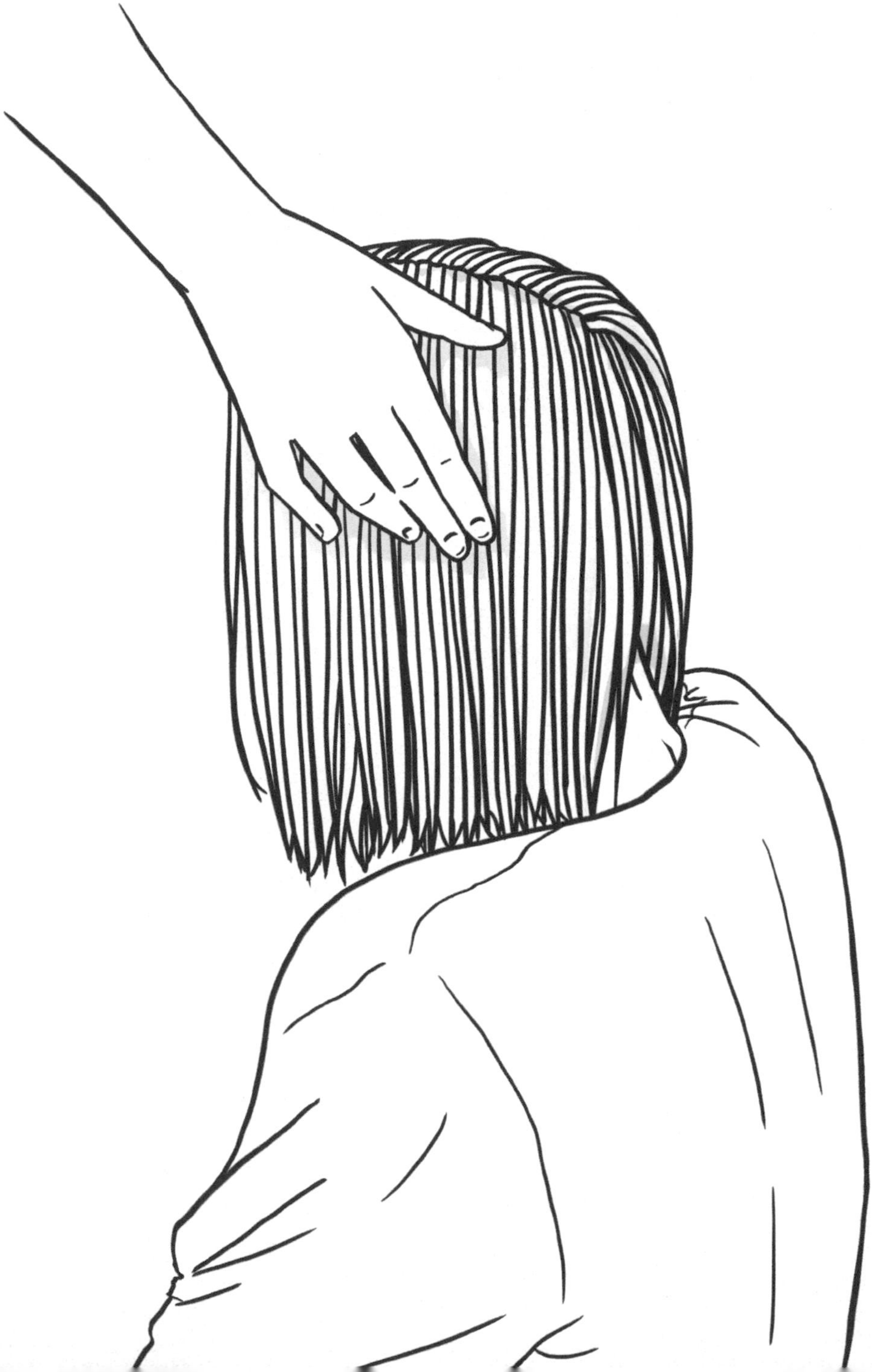

do not give a man
more of yourself than
what he has
to offer.

you are so much
more than pretty. you
are beautiful, brave,
intelligent, and strong.

women are not
complicated,
they just need
to know you
care.

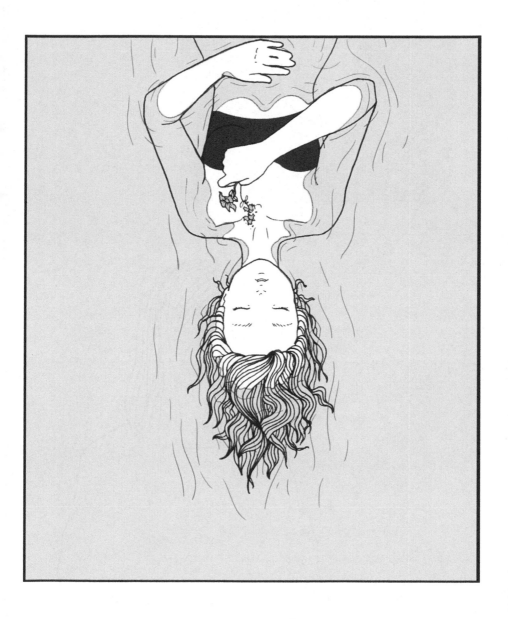

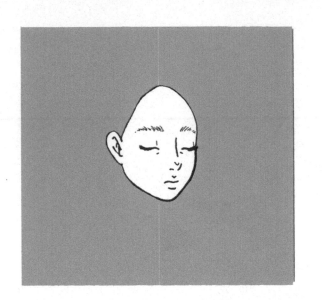

she just wants
you to show her
through actions
more than words.

find a man who
treats you as his
everything.

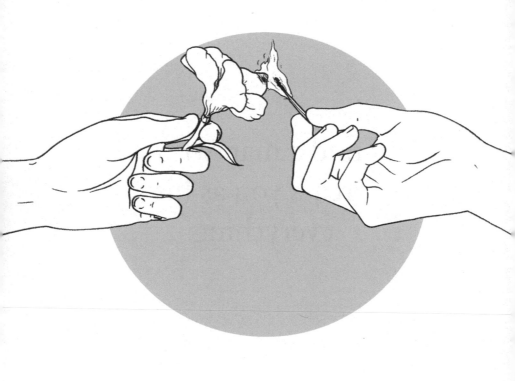

don't let him
keep you there
if he's not willing
to stay.

you are my
most beautiful
someone.

"i remember you and it makes me cry.
i let you go and let the world have you.
i wish i could have known people don't stay the same forever.
what has the world made you believe?
please, tell me, so i can remind you of everything you are.
tell me when a hug was nothing more.
and a kiss, was only a kiss.
and when a man taking you out
didn't oblige you to anything.
i know you are in there somewhere.
i remember. i remember, because we sat on your porch as kids
and told the world how everything in this life is beautiful,
and i couldn't help but think this life isn't as beautiful as you.
i thought, "she is going to conquer the world; nothing will stop her."
and then i saw those boys, those stupid boys,
take your heart, one after the next.
and i didn't do anything to stop them.
i am sorry, i am so sorry. i don't think i'll ever be able to forgive myself.
it's those very moments i wish i could take back.
it's those very moments i wish i was there.
to protect a girl. a girl that... was special to me..."

i want to be the one
to make you feel like
you just experienced
love for the first
time.

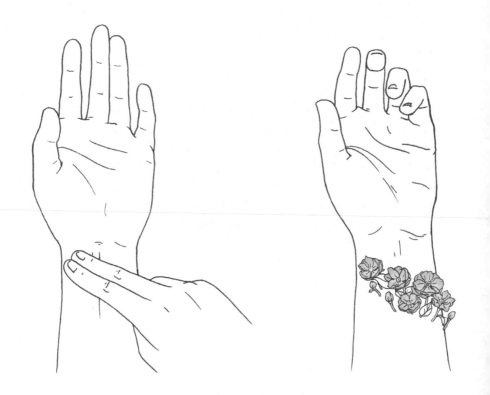

i guess i just want to address something. ladies, there are men out there who will love deeper than you could ever imagine. yes, are they few and between, certainly, but they do exist. don't give up on such a love and don't settle for less. find a man who loves you for more than your body, or how you wear your make-up, or how pretty you look in the mirror. you deserve that. you don't deserve someone who just uses your heart and makes you feel empty inside. it's a terrible feeling and makes you feel less and less that love really exists. you start feeling not as beautiful, and not as worthy, and you forget how freaking beautiful you really are. and it hurts. it hurts to start feeling that way. you know? and you just want him to start seeing you the way you thought he saw you, until you realize he never saw you that way. and in your head you were just wanting everything to be fine because you love him. but then you realize, you have to move on from something that was never working, but it hurts, it hurts so much. and you feel your whole world is crashing around you. and you don't know what to do. you don't know whether to give up or keep going. to trust someone with your heart again or keep it close to you. it's just all emptiness inside. but you know there's someone out there who doesn't plan on using your heart against you. someone who plans on treating you right. you just have to find him. that's all... that's all.

you are, and
maybe i say this
too much, truly
special to me.

can i just tell you
i love you very much,
and that i wish
you were here.

she loved
and he never
cared.

"i remember him telling me that he loves me. i remember him tell-
ing me that i was his everything, and i'm all that mattered. and then
it all died. i gave him my heart and he just crushed it. he shattered
it to a million pieces. and i don't know why. i don't know why he did
that? i thought everything was fine, he told me it was. and now i
don't. i don't know what to feel. it just hurts, you know? and i think
it was love, i think it was something special, but now i just don't
know. i want to find love, i don't want to be alone, but i don't feel like
going through this again. it's like pouring your heart out and then
it's just used up. i can't. i can't have this happen to me again. it feels
like i'm dying inside. it just hurts so much..."
"you'll meet someone again."
"...i've heard that one before. no, i won't. or maybe i will. i don't know.
it's just hard to think right now. i don't care, that's how i feel. i mean,
how could he? i don't understand. i don't get it. to ruin everything.
and it's not even that he cheated, it's the fact he lied to me. he lied
straight to my face and he expects me to trust him again. the crazy
thing is, i was even thinking about it. that's how much i love him.
but is that even love anymore or is it just me trying to hold onto
something?"
"you deserve someone who is going to treat you like their every-
thing, not one who is going to take advantage of your heart..."
"you're right... you're right..."

somewhere out there
is someone waiting to
love you the way you were
meant to be loved.

i hope you find someone
who doesn't make you
feel replaceable.

you deserve more
than being hurt
by the person you
think loves you.

"i don't know. i guess i wanted to love. to fall deeply in love with you, but it seems you've found someone else. and i won't lie, my heart hurts, but seeing you happy is all i've ever wanted. and i think if it came down it, that's all i want for you. to see you smile, and to see you laugh, and to see you dance at the thought of life again, like we used to when we were kids. everything was beautiful back then. i don't know where the time goes. i really don't. i just wish we could have some of it back. maybe life wouldn't be so hard. just promise me, you'll be all right? and if there's anything, you ever need, i'll be here."

"i know. i know you will. you know i love you... it's just hard feeling like you love someone, but you're trapped loving someone else..."

"what are you saying..."

"what i am saying is... i really can't do this right now. please, don't make me do this. you know i love you, and i will always love you, but sometimes things aren't meant to be. sometimes, the world chooses for you, and sometimes..."

"sometimes what?"

"please... don't... just don't do it. don't make me see you sad. you have everything beautiful in this life you want. don't let it be put all on me. live. be free. be beautiful. you deserve that. you deserve so much more than me. i'm sorry. i'm sorry, for catching your heart, and feeling like i let you down. i'm sorry, i wasn't there for you, when you needed me, and i'm sorry that things ended up this way... i'm just so sorry..."

my love, somedays we'll
fight and not all nights
we'll agree, but in the
end it is you and always
you i'll love.

don't let him
make you feel crazy
for the things he
put you through.

when i fell in love
with you, i fell in
love with all of you,
everything about
you.

i love you for you,
i wouldn't want
anyone different
in my life.

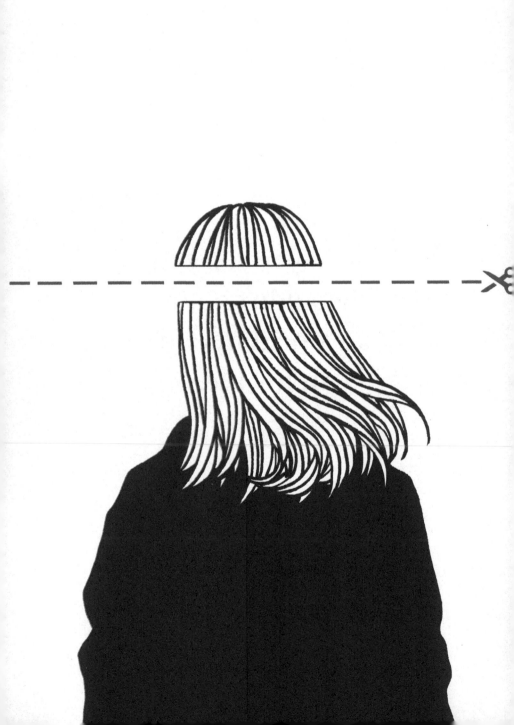

a man who really
cares, won't make
excuses.

even a
strong woman
gets tired.

"sometimes, she just needs you to kiss her on the cheek, and tell her she is beautiful. sometimes, she just needs to know you care enough to be ready and on time. sometimes, she will need you, not for advice, but to hold her close to your chest, so she can listen to your heartbeat. she's strong, but everyone has their breaking point. she wants a man who can turn her weaknesses into strength, not someone who chastises her for not being good enough, but someone who lifts her up when she's about to fall. she wants a man ready to fight for her, not because he has too, but because he's willing to give up everything to make sure she's ok. he doesn't have to be perfect either, hell she doesn't expect him to be, but she expects him to be honest. to tell the truth even when it hurts, because she would rather live in fear than in denial. she doesn't want a lot a things, just enough to know that she matters. to know that even when you might disagree, at least she knows she's been heard. and if you give her these things i promise you she will give you everything in return. sometimes, even more than is given back. why? because she will love you, and she will love you deeply, enough to move the stars and the ends of the earth. she will love you even when everyone else disagrees. because by showing her these things it proves to her you are the man she always thought you would be."

block his number.
delete his texts.
move on.
be happy.

darling, soon
enough he
will be just a
memory.

i want to love
you for the rest
of my life. is that
all right?

forgive him.
it is time to
let go.

forgive yourself,
you didn't know
he would hurt
you.

she'll never
forget the way
you treated
her.

she didn't love
the wrong way,
she loved the
wrong one.

i want you to
continue being
the absolute best
part of my life.

just because you
break doesn't
mean you are
broken.

if he doesn't
make you feel
beautiful, he's
not the one.

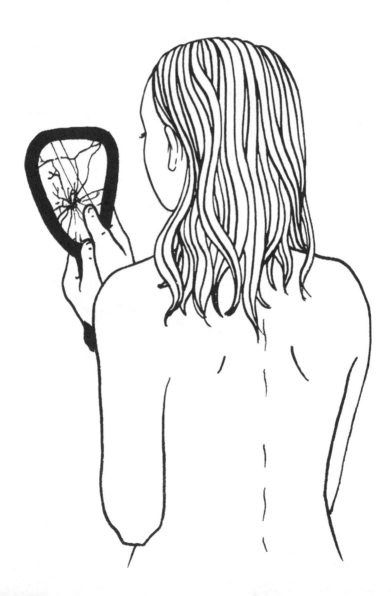

find a man
who doesn't make
you feel you are
hard to love.

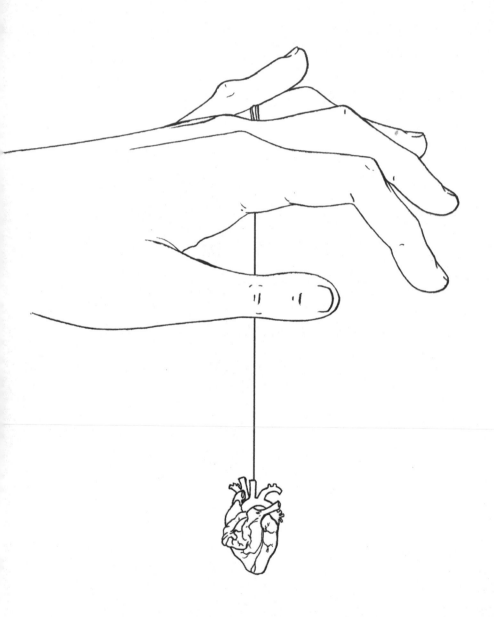

you are
all my heart
needs.

listen to her,
even when she
isn't speaking.

treat her like
she is the world, and
she will give you
the world.

you are
beautifully perfect
the way you
are.

you are
everything to
me. you always
will be.

hey, i just wanted to
say, i love you, and
i hope you have a
day as beautiful
as you.

i think you already know
this, but you're beautiful.
everyday of every year
you're the prettiest,
kindest, sweetest person
i know.

"and so i gave my body
to him.
it was in pieces she said.
bloody and bruised.
like our love had been
beaten too many
times
to feel another touch of his.
so, she sat there
with her eyes wide open
as her lips met
his.
and she became numb.
but much too heavy
to breathe.
she pushed him away.
but he kept
going.
again.
again.
and again.
until she felt
she had been
stripped
away.
until her soul
had met his
in some dark
place

where they
whisper
"well, it was only once
upon a time".
but there is never
an ending.
because in all that darkness.
in all that imagery.
it is him.
like she is
no longer her
own woman.
like she is cut
torn.
stripped.
battered.
and bruised.
and in that
moment
gasping
for air,
she came back
to him saying,
"hello,
my
love."

if he loves
you, he will
make the
effort.

just don't tell
her that you love
her, show her
that you do.

i miss you very much
and you are in my
thoughts each and
every day.

you must understand
her before you
can truly love her.

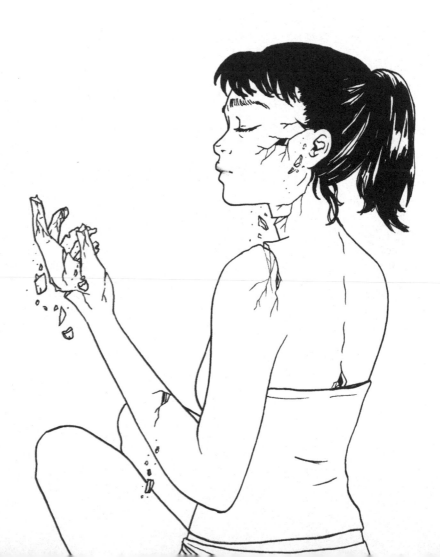

you must get to know her. that's the fastest way for a wom-
an to love you. she wants you to get to know her heart, she
wants you to know what lies beneath the surface of her skin.
she doesn't want another person who uses her heart without
knowing how valuable and precious it is. she wants someone
who will protect it and protect it well. when she is hurting,
she wants someone who will protect her from all the awful
and terrible things she might be feeling. but she doesn't want
your sympathy. she wants your strength. your resilience. that
fire in your eye that you get when something or someone is
precious to you. and if you learn to protect a woman's heart
she will always feel safe with you. but if you don't get to learn
a woman's heart, you will never learn all the beautiful things
that make her the person who she is. and that love will remain
fragile. it will remain easy to break and easy to let go. and if a
man doesn't want to get to know your heart, well ladies, that's
the first sign you should go because a man who doesn't want
to get know all the beautiful things that make you who you
are isn't the man for you. and trust me, the most beautiful
thing a man will find in his life is the heart of a woman who
loves him. but he must learn. he must cherish it. and he must
allow time to grow.

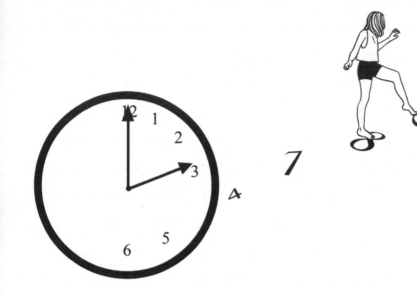

he's not
worth
your time.

"find a man who is willing to take the time out of his day to be there for you. find a man that you feel safe with, that feels like home to you. don't settle for less, because i'm telling you, darling, there will come a day when you look back and ask yourself why i wasted my time on someone who didn't love me. why wasn't i strong enough to let go, to move on forward with someone who wouldn't break my heart a million times. you'll ask yourself these questions, and before you know it will be too late. your heart will have broken more than times than it is able to love. when a man touches you it should feel gentle, when he tells you he loves you those words should feel kind. they should feel like you were meant to be together, not that you're trying to hold onto something from being torn apart. when he looks you in the eyes, ask yourself, do you trust him. and i don't mean just that simple trust that you have for most people, but that deep and powerful trust that is rare for a person to bring out of you."

he isn't worth
the pain.
you have to
let him go.

she just wants
someone who loves
her as much as she
loves him.

i've never
needed someone
before i met
you.

don't give up
your life for him
knowing he will
never love you.

being savage is
what makes her
beautiful.

when someone cares for
you deeply, always
remember, you are holding
two hearts instead of
one.

if he truly loved
you, he wouldn't be
messing around with
other girls.

she gave
everything of herself until there
was nothing left
to give
left
to pieces
by the person
she thought
loved her.
she didn't stop
to think
but she knew
she couldn't stay because this
wasn't the first time
her heart had
been broken.
it had been many times but every time she felt deep
down in her heart maybe he would change. but she
knew.
she knew the love
they felt for each other was different.
and eventually
as much as
it hurt her
she had to let
him go.
she knew
that holding on
would only hurt
her.
and as much
as she knew
it didn't make
it any easier to say good-bye.

your smile
is the most
beautiful thing
to me.

i never want to
see you hurting.
i want to be able
to take all the
pain away.

everything that has
happened we can put
behind us now, you
have me, and i have
you.

"when i said love
you,
at first the words
caught in my throat,
we were speechless
and maybe
a little bit scared,
but that didn't stop you
from saying,
"i love you" back.
i feel there is a
moment
when you're willing to risk every-
thing with someone
and you were
willing to risk that moment with
me.
see in you,
well i see the
most beautiful person
in the world.
i know there are
days when
we fight and there
are times when
we just want
to throw it all
away,
but there is
never a day
i stop loving you.
you keep something
whole in my heart
i never knew was
broken.
i wish to love you,
i wish to cherish you,
and i wish to keep loving you.
i have never met someone
like
you.
i truly love you,
with all my
heart."

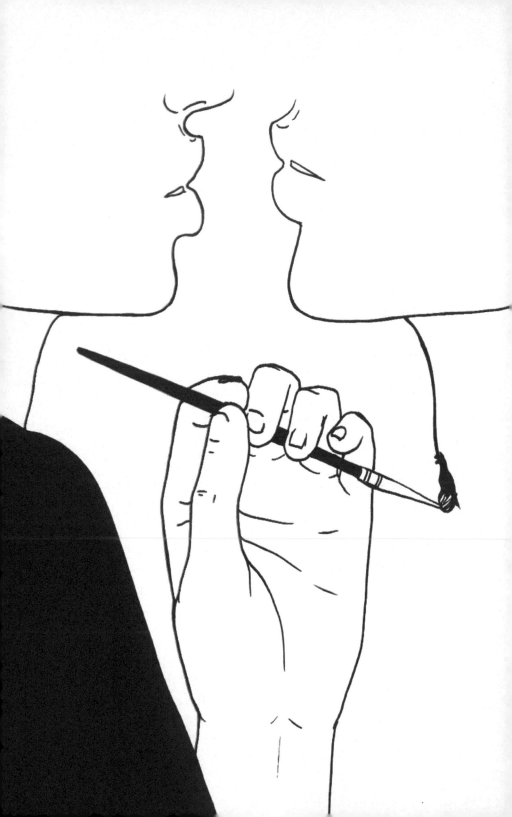

loving someone else
is easy, learning
to love yourself is
the hard part.

you were a beautiful
stranger, i loved
you before we even
said hello.

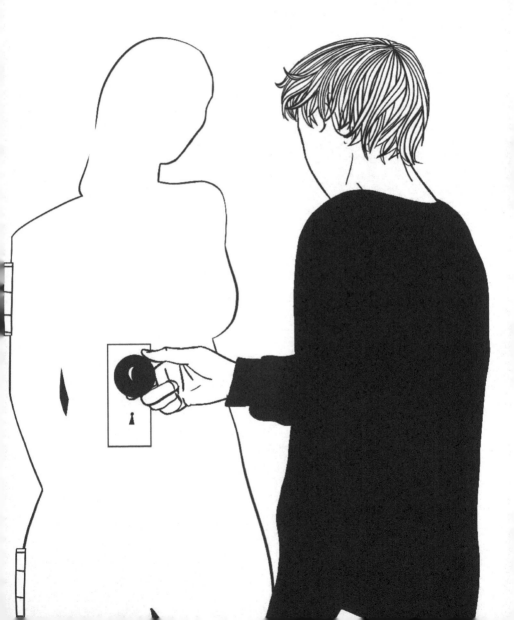

treat her well.
she's rare.

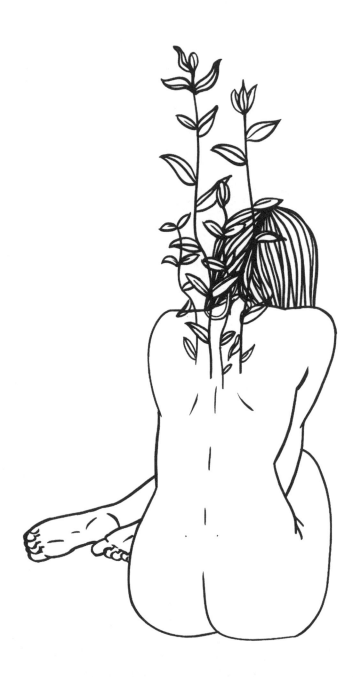

if your man says, "you don't
deserve me, you deserve better"

it's a warning, it means you're
about to get hurt.

find a man who
makes you feel
loved everyday.

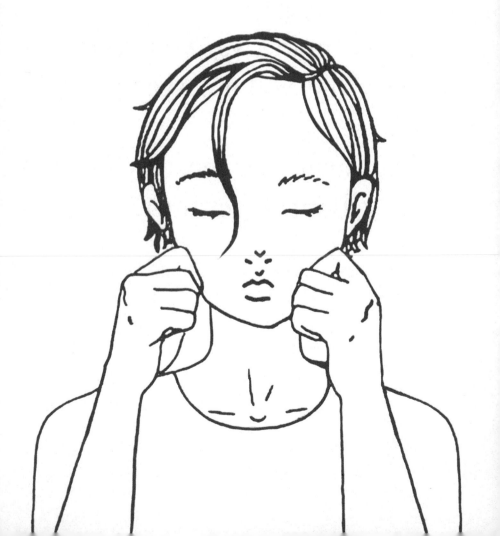

"find a man who respects you. who values you. who doesn't treat you as an inconvenience. who finds you beautiful on days even when you don't. who cares about you. who will be there to pick you up when you fall. who will hold your hand through all the struggles and all the worries and everything that makes you feel unwhole. because you are whole. you are beautiful. you are brave. and you deserve a man who treats you as such. you deserve a man who values you with all his heart. that's what you deserve."

to the woman reading this
don't let him take you
for granted.

"i didn't know my relationship would end like this, i just feel so sad..."
"hey, listen to me. you will find somebody who takes the time to
make you feel loved. who appreciates you. and everything that you
are. i don't even think you realize how beautiful you are. to say it as
it is, i look at you and i see a woman who has everything to give. and
nothing to be ashamed of. you are so strong. and you are so beautiful.
you are so brave. and i know the things that you have had to put up
with in this world. and i know how hard it has been for you. but i'm
letting you know, i will always be there for you. i promise. so please,
don't be sad... don't be sad. you know i miss your smile, that smile
that you have. haha, yes that smile! you know, one day you are going
to meet the perfect person, someone who treats you like you are
everything in the world."
"how about if i never find that person?"
"you will find that person. i know in my heart of hearts you will. you
just have to give it time. and don't give up on love because there are
many people that love you."
"you love me..."
"yeah... yeah i guess i do."
#conversation

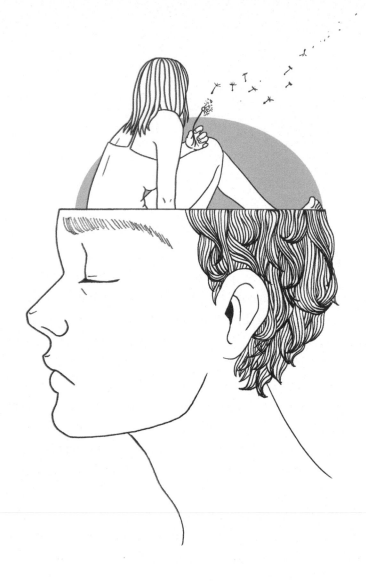

find a man who
makes you his priority.

"find a man who says i love you each and every day. find a man who is not afraid to tell you when he is wrong. find a man who cares about you with all his heart. because darling, there will come a day, when you ask yourself did i truly experience love. and when that moment comes i want you to be able to say yes. yes i did. and i have no regrets. because there is nothing worse than at the end of it all telling yourself maybe you could have done something different. maybe you could have fought a little harder, to find a man who will tell you how beautiful you are each and every day."

you deserve to be
with a man who
treats you right.

a woman like you deserves everything.

"hey, you, beautiful what are you crying about?"

"i just want someone to love me the way i love them... i just keep getting hurt over

and over

and over again."

"darling, you will find someone. you don't worry about that... i know you will..."

"but how about if i never find someone? how about if i just end up alone?"

(he placed his hand on her shoulder)

"hey, you have me. we may not be lovers, but you have me for anything. if you are

ever feeling sad

or depressed just come talk to me. i'll listen."

"i appreciate that. i know you do. and i am so grateful to you."

(she looked sadly at the ground. he began to talk)

"hey do you remember the day we first met? you were sitting by yourself and i

thought you were the most beautiful girl in the world."

"you thought i was beautiful?"

"yeah i did and i still do."

(she reached for his hand. and they looked at each other for awhile)

"there is something about you that makes me always want to be with you. to pro-

tect you. to love

you. i can't explain it really, but it's a feeling that i can't let go."

"i feel the same way... i just... i never knew."

(and he began to cry)

"i promise. i will be there for you, darling. i promise you... with all my heart."

dear women,
you are more
than enough.

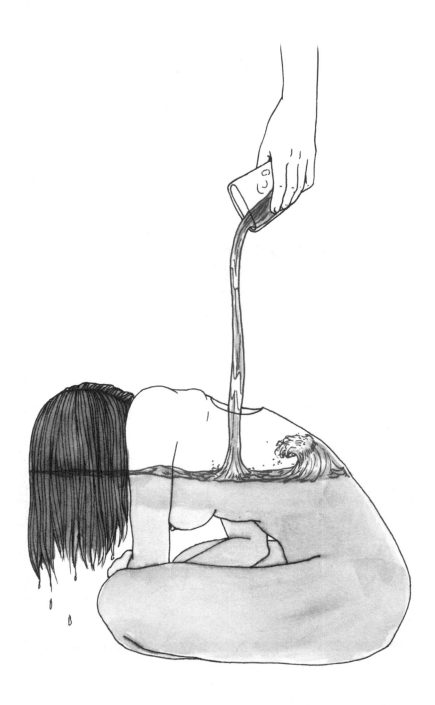

she saved herself,
leaving him.

"and i told him that there was only so much left of me to give because my heart had been broken too many times. he just smiled, telling me, how he would never break my heart. and i believed him. he would wake up. and tell me how beautiful i am. how i meant the world to him. how stupid was i. to give myself so vulnerably again to someone who i really believed loved me. i heard him in the room whispering, "hey, beautiful". i stood there. frozen. that as soon as i opened that door, my heart would just break completely, but he didn't deserve that."

"deserve what?"

"to see how deeply and madly i had fallen in love with him."

strong woman, you
deserve to be loved.

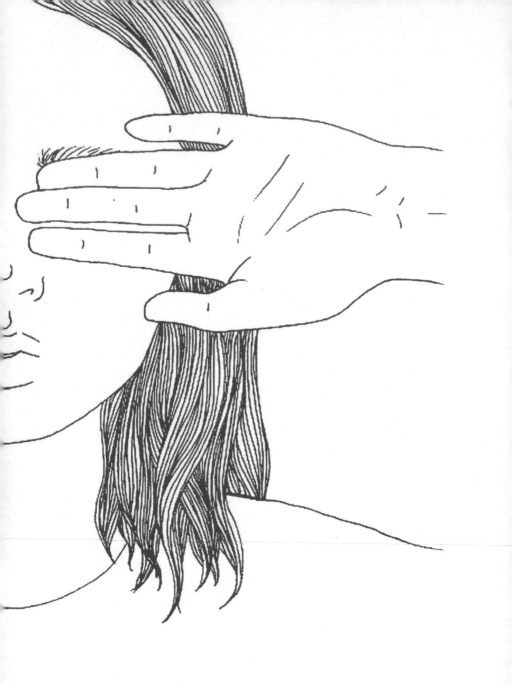

she realized she deserved better.

you are a rare woman
bold, beautiful, and
fierce.

he doesn't love
you, he just
likes the idea
of being with you.

she became strong without him.

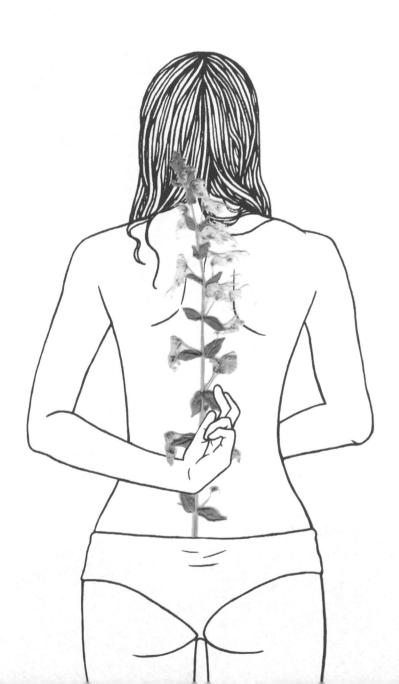

she found herself without him.

go to sleep, he doesn't deserve you.

it's really simple
a man who loves you
will be there for you.

my dear, you're still
here, but i feel we
said goodbye such
a long time ago.

you deserve someone who
doesn't make you change
who you are, who loves you,
and all your faults.

there is never a day i love
you less and there are days
where i think i cannot
possibly love you more, but
i am proven wrong time
and time again.

i never stopped
loving you, i just
needed some time
for myself.

and finally she chose herself.

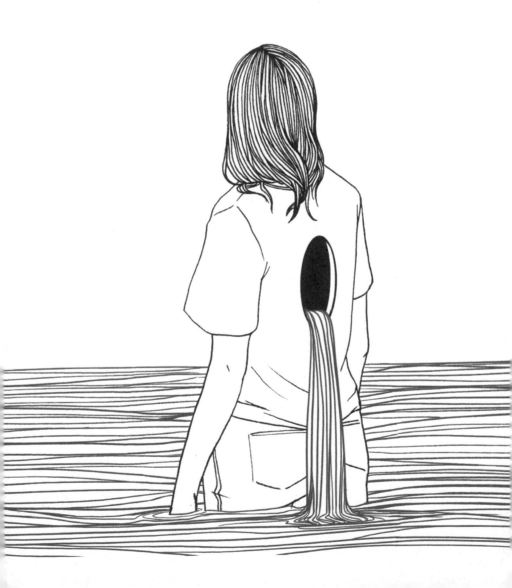

EZANA SALGADO
Author

Ezana is twenty-seven years old and a Santa Barbara native. Between the ages of fifteen and twenty-five, he spent time in over seven residential treatment programs for Obsessive Compulsive Disorder. In addition to his own healing journey, he was witness to the profound struggles of his fellow patients—particularly young women—who had formidable trauma histories and never saw the beauty, strength, and resilience in themselves that appeared to Ezana. Writing, which had always been an outlet for him, became Ezana's tribute to the bravery he saw, and to the great strength within all women. Ezana's work creates a world of love, tranquility, and peace for women and girls who are hurting and feel apart from the beauty of the world around them. His Instagram following has grown to over 83,000 people, and his work has reached millions worldwide.

INSTAGRAM: @EZANASALGADO_

ELLIANA ESQUIVEL
Illustrator

Elliana is a self-taught illustrator based in Charlotte, North Carolina. Elliana's minimalist work blends traditional and digital mediums to communicate a spectrum of human emotions through delicate linework and simple color schemes. Growing up as a dual citizen of America and the Philippines, Elliana remains greatly influenced by both her East Asian and Western heritage. Elliana has illustrated book covers for Harper Collins; Little, Brown and Company; and Faber and Faber, as well as album artwork for two-time Grammy winner Tori Kelly. Artistic since childhood, she began working in the industry at 16. Elliana plans on pursuing a degree in animation in the future.

INSTAGRAM: @ELESQ

Made in the USA
Coppell, TX
20 December 2022

90351320R00105